For Childhood Friends Everywhere

Paper Republic LLC

7548 Ravenna Ave NE, Seattle, Washington 98115

Text and illustration copyright © 2014 by Wenzheng Fu

English translation copyright © 2016 by China Educational Publications Import & Export Corporation Ltd.

English edition copyright © 2016 by China Educational Publications Import & Export Corporation Ltd.

Publication Consultant: Roxanne Hsu Feldman

Published by Paper Republic LLC, by arrangement with Zhejiang Juvenile and Children's Publishing House Co., Ltd.

All rights reserved, including the right of reproduction in whole or in part in any form.

Printed and bound in China.

ISBN 978-1-945-29511-9

The illustrations in this book were rendered in gouache.

For more titles from Candied Plums and additional features, please visit www.candiedplums.com.

Buddy Is So Annoying

by Wenzheng Fu

translated by Adam Lanphier

Candied Plums

I've known Buddy since the first day of kindergarten.

I think he's so annoying.

He's annoying when he can't keep up.

He's also annoying when he's faster than me.

He's annoying when he talks.

And more annoying when
he doesn't talk.

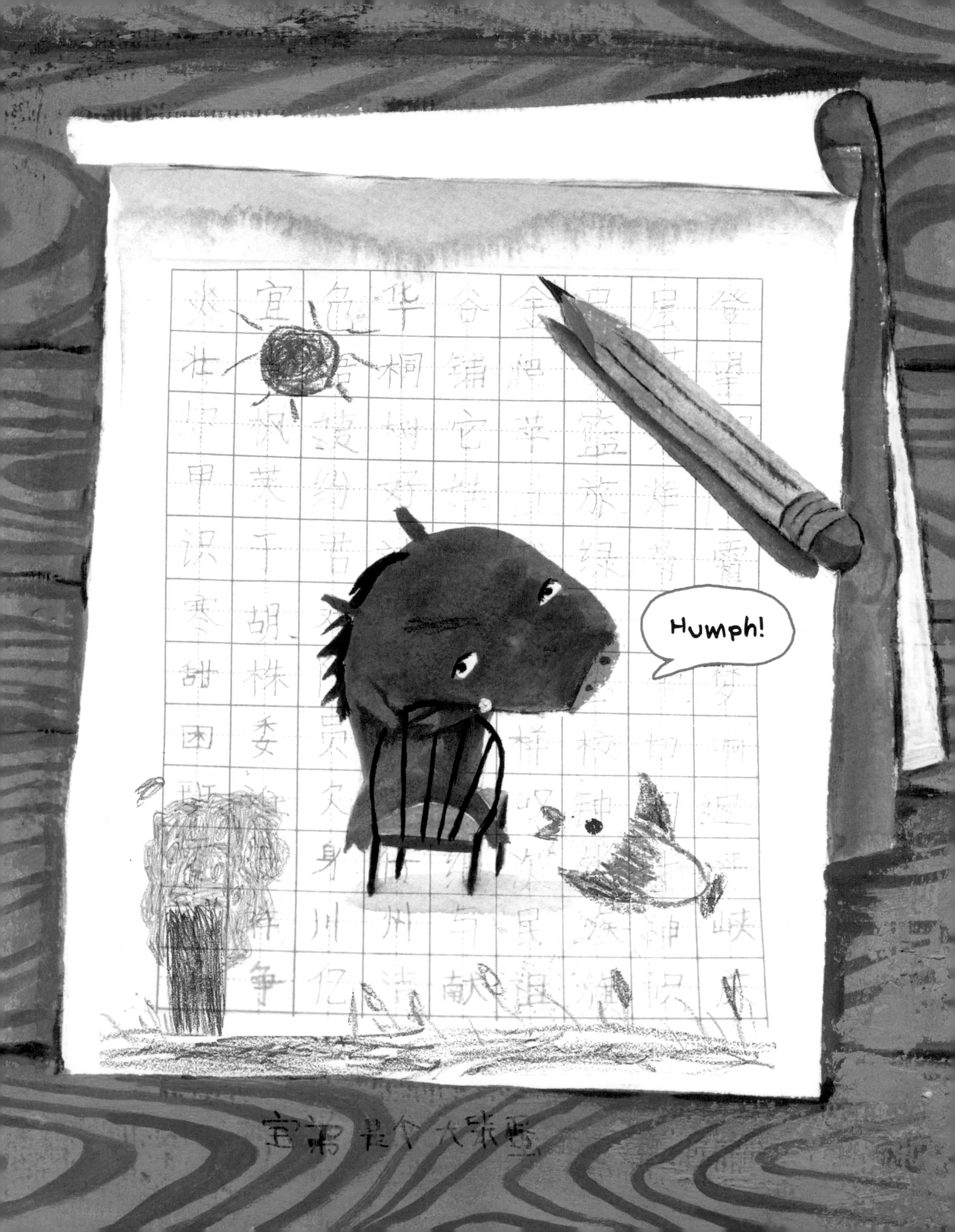
Humph!

Once in a while, I forget how annoying he is.

But on the whole, he's definitely annoying.

·

··

···

He really bugs me.

.

..

...

But once in a while, being bugged isn't so bad.

I only let him hang
around when I have to.

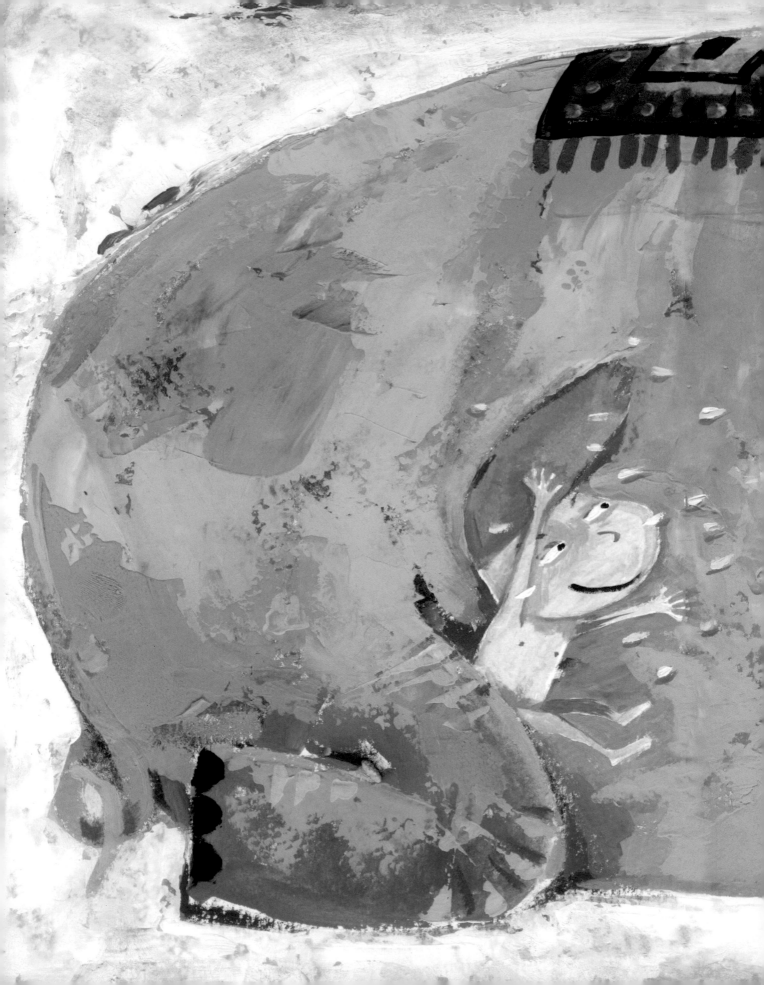

And I only play with him when I have to.

But then, before I know it, we'll have been playing
for a long time.

But this doesn't change the fact that Buddy is annoying.

The way he looks when he's not talking
is still so annoying…

And when he talks, it's as annoying as ever.

The waves here are three stories tall!

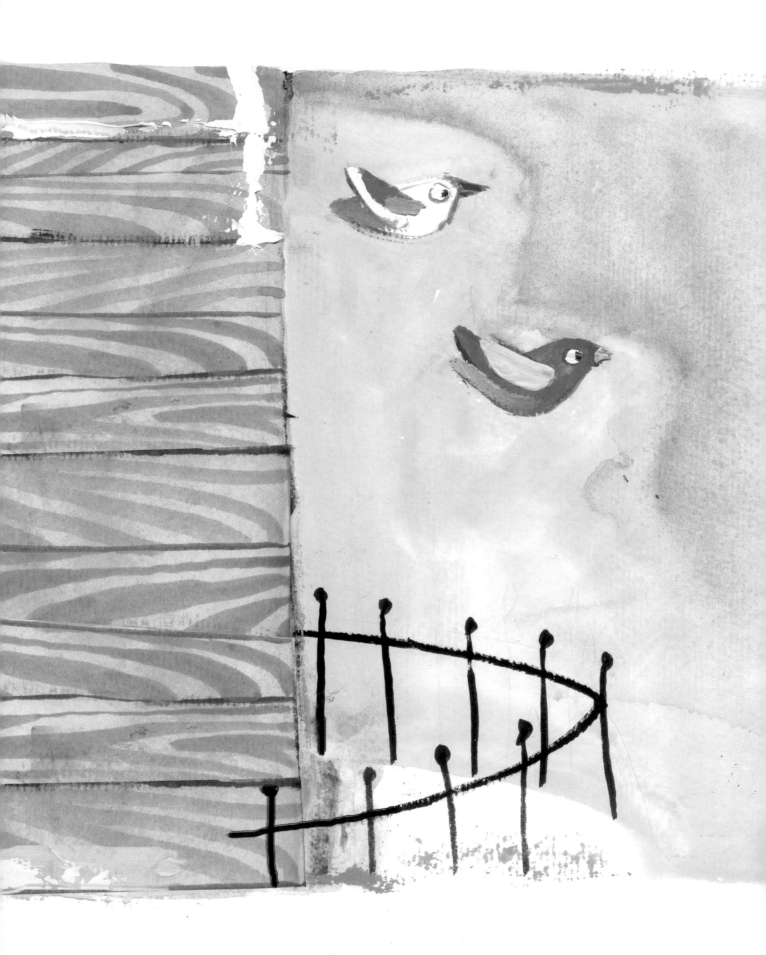

Man, he is so annoying when he's early! Haha!

It's just that I sometimes forget to be annoyed.

For a long time after that, I let Buddy hang around.
Does that mean he doesn't annoy me?

Nope! He still annoys me. But do you know what? Having someone around to keep you company and annoy you is a wonderful thing.